MICR😈MONSTERS

MICROSCOPIC LIFE UP CLOSE

MICROMONSTERS

IN YOUR BODY

Clare Hibbert

PowerKiDS
press

Published in 2017 by
The Rosen Publishing Group, Inc.
29 East 21st Street, New York, NY 10010

Cataloging-in-Publication Data
Names: Hibbert, Clare.
Title: Micromonsters in your body / Clare Hibbert.
Description: New York : PowerKids Press, 2017. | Series: Micromonsters: microscopic life up close | Includes index.
Identifiers: ISBN 9781508150886 (pbk.) | ISBN 9781508150848 (library bound) | ISBN 9781508150763 (6 pack)
Subjects: LCSH: Human body--Microbiology--Juvenile literature.
Classification: LCC QR171.A1 H53 2017 | DDC 612--d23

Copyright © 2017 Franklin Watts, a division of Hachette Children's Group

Series editor: Paul Humphrey
Series designer: sprout.uk.com
Planning and production by Discovery Books Limited
Design and illustration: sprout.uk.com

Photo credits: Alamy: cover (SGO/BSIP SA), 1 (The Science Picture Company), 3 (Science Photo Library), 4–5 (Scott Camazine), 8–9 (Science Photo Library), 14–15 (Science Photo Library) 16–17 (The Science Picture Company), 20–21 (Mediscan), 22–23 (Scott Camazine), 28–29 (PHOTOTAKE Inc.); Bigstock: 4bl (Ilike), 5r (Jody Ann), 6bl (HighwayStarz), 7br (I Candy), 8l (Yulia), 13br (Marmion), 15r (ryelo357), 16l (Timurpix), 18tr (animaxx3d), 19r (natulrich), 20br (PixelsAway), 22br (_jure), 24bl (maxim ibragimov), 26tr (rukawa), 29bl (Hummy); Getty: 6–7 (Media for Medical); Science Photo Library: 10–11, 12–13, 18–19 (NIAID/National Institutes of Health), 24–25 (David McCarthy), 26–27 (Eye of Science); sprout.uk.com: 31; Wikimedia Commons: 10bl (Tanalai), 27tl (James Heilman, MD), 28bl (CDC/Janice Haney Carr).

Manufactured in the United States of America
CPSIA Compliance Information: Batch #BS16PK: For Further Information contact Rosen Publishing, New York, New York at 1-800-237-9932

Note to the reader: many SEM images use false colors to make the subject more visible.
Whenever possible the magnification of images has been added.

CONTENTS

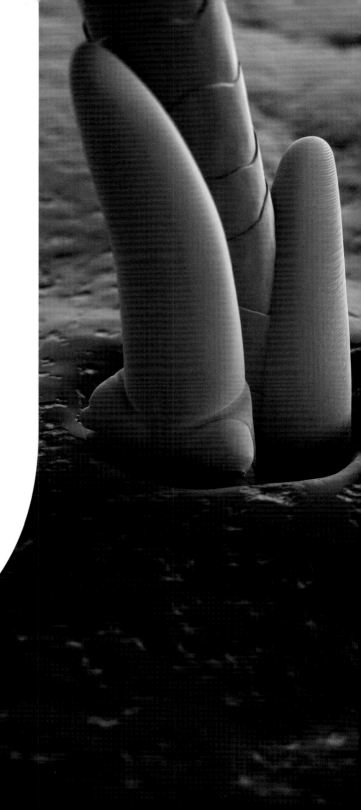

Words in **bold** can be found in
the glossary on page 30.

THE WORLD OF MICROMONSTERS

Did you know you're never truly alone? Your body is a habitat for millions of little living things ... they're on your skin, in your blood and even in your tummy. Your body is a world of micromonsters!

Tiny living things that you can see only under a microscope are called **microorganisms**. Some of them are microanimals: insects and other creatures too small to see without a microscope. Other organisms are **microbes**: micro**fungi** (members of the mushroom family), **bacteria** and **viruses** so tiny that you need super strong microscopes to see them.

Scanning electron microscopes (SEMs) can magnify things many thousands of times. Let's look at some of the body micromonsters that SEMs can show us.

Even ordinary microscopes (not SEMs) can now magnify objects up to 1,024 times. They have bright lighting and multiple lenses.

MONSTROUS DATA

Name	Giardia
Latin name	*Giardia lamblia*
Adult length	10–20 **micrometers** (see pg. 31)
Habitat	Mammals' **intestines**
Lifespan	Up to 30 days

A Giardia parasite seen through an SEM

GHASTLY GIARDIA

A good place to start in the world of body micromonsters is with some nasty little **parasites** called Giardia. They get into people's bodies through drinking water and live in their intestines, causing diarrhea, stomach cramps and nausea (feeling sick). At this stage of their life, they have whiplike tails, called flagella, that help them swim. As they pass out of the body, they lose the tails and become hardy blobs, called cysts. Giardia cysts can survive in cold water. Giardia infects around 280,000 people around the world each year.

Giardia parasites target other animals besides humans. They're such a big problem for beavers that infection, properly called giardiasis, is sometimes known as "beaver fever"!

GROSS OR WHAT?

The diarrhea you get if you have Giardia parasites onboard is very distinctive — pale, yellowish and oily. Eww!

Flagellum

ITCHY NITS

Just thinking about these little passengers makes your head itch and your hand creep up to your scalp to scratch. Most of us get head lice at some time in our lives.

Head lice are a kind of insect that live on human scalps and feed on blood. These parasites can't fly, jump or swim, but they can crawl or climb from head to head. They can also survive off the scalp for up to 48 hours — a good excuse not to share combs, brushes or towels with your brother, sister or friend.

MONSTROUS HABITAT

Combing through the hair shows the egg cases.

MONSTROUS DATA

Name	Head louse
Latin name	*Pediculus humanus capitis*
Adult length	2.5 mm
Habitat	Human scalp
Lifespan	3 weeks

Teenagers have started getting more lice because of the fashion for taking selfies—they put their heads together to take the pictures!

LOUSY LIFE CYCLE

A female head louse glues her eggs close to the hair root where your toasty body heat will keep them warm. After about a week the eggs hatch into **nymphs**, leaving behind the stuck-on egg case, which is called a nit. Head lice go through three nymph stages before they reach adulthood. They molt (shed their skin) between each stage. Within hours of becoming an adult, a head louse can **mate** and the female can produce eggs.

Eyes on developing embryo

Human hair

Egg case

Head lice only affect humans—but chimps have their own very similar **species** of louse.

GROSS OR WHAT?

In extreme head lice **infestations**, there can be thousands of lice. They form sticky nests and the hair gets glued together.

IN YOUR FACE

Eyelash mites are tiny, parasitic mites that live on humans — mostly on our face. They belong to the arachnid family, but they are much skinnier than their spider cousins.

Eyelash mites live in and around our eyelashes, eyebrows and nose hairs. These micromonsters burrow down into our follicles — the holes from which our hairs grow. Inside the follicles are the special **glands** that produce sebum, the oily, waxy substance that waterproofs our skin and makes our hair greasy if we forget to wash it. Sebum is one of an eyelash mite's favorite foods. Its other favorite is dead skin **cells** — YUCK!

MONSTROUS HABITAT

Everyone has eyelash mites — the older you are, the more you are likely to have.

Hair follicle

An artwork of eyelash mites crawling across skin

An average adult is **host** to between 1,000 and 2,000 eyelash mites!

MONSTROUS DATA

Name	Eyelash mite
Latin name	*Demodex*
Adult length	0.3–0.4 mm
Habitat	Hair follicles and sebaceous glands
Lifespan	Several weeks

MATING MITES

When a mite wants a mate, she takes a stroll across the skin — a super-slow stroll, as her top speed is only about 1 cm an hour! Aftter finding a male and mating, she lays eggs inside a follicle or sebaceous (sebum-producing) gland. Six-legged **larvae** hatch a few days later, and within a week they've changed into their eight-legged adult form.

GROSS OR WHAT?

A German doctor called Gustav Simon discovered eyelash mites in 1841. He was looking at his patients' pus-filled pimples under a microscope.

Eyelash mites are harmless, but some people are allergic to their saliva and break out in pimples.

WEEPY PEEPERS

If your eyes turn pink or red you may have a condition called conjunctivitis. Your eyes might become sticky and weepy, too. Sometimes the cause is an allergy; more usually it's bacteria or a virus.

Viruses are microbes that **reproduce** by making exact copies of themselves. To do this, they need to be inside the living cell of an animal, plant or bacterium. A few different viruses can result in conjunctivitis. They include the cold and flu viruses (see pages 14–15), as well as HSV-1, best known for causing cold sores — itchy, scabby wounds around the mouth.

MONSTROUS HABITAT

The thin skin over the white of the eye is called the conjunctiva — any condition that irritates this is called conjunctivitis.

MONSTROUS DATA

Name	Cold sore virus
Latin name	*Herpes simplex virus 1*
Adult length	100 **nanometers** (see page 31)
Habitat	Living cells
Lifespan	Its host's lifespan, or 15 minutes outside a host

GROSS OR WHAT?

In conjunctivitis caused by bacteria, the eyes produce sticky yellow or green gunk – sometimes enough to form a thick crust that seals the eyes shut.

PASSING IT ON

HSV-1 is passed on through spit. You might think you're safe so long as you don't go around kissing everyone, but unfortunately HSV-1 is very infectious. You can get it just by taking a sip from someone else's drink. Conjunctivitis from bacteria is easy to pass on, too. The best way to avoid catching it or passing it on is to wash your hands frequently, especially before eating.

Human body cells (blue) infected with HSV-1 (round and pink)

About two-thirds of people under 50 are infected with HSV-1. Once you are infected with HSV-1, you have it for life.

MOUTH MONSTERS

Everyone knows it's good to brush your teeth twice a day. But what exactly are you brushing away — and what life forms still lurk in your mouth even when your teeth feel squeaky clean?

The bad news is that your mouth is swarming with microbes. It's wet and warm — just what they like — so they are constantly multiplying. The good news is that regular tooth brushing keeps these bacteria under control, so that they live in perfect balance with you and each other.

There are up to 200 different species of bacteria in your mouth right now!

GROSS OR WHAT?

When bacteria and saliva work together to break down food particles in your mouth, they produce yucky-smelling gases ... in other words, stinky breath!

MONSTROUS DATA

Name	Mouth germs
Latin name	*Streptococcus*
Adult length	0.5 micrometers
Habitat	Mouth, throat, lungs, nose
Lifespan	Constantly dividing and multiplying

GOOD, BAD OR BOTH?

Streptococcus is one of the main bacteria in your mouth — and most of the time it does a helpful job. The acids it produces kill harmful germs and fungi that could cause disease. But sometimes the balance tips. If the *Streptococcus* is multiplying fast, it will produce too much acid. This acid wears away the protective coating on your teeth and starts to rot them. False teeth, anyone? Other *Streptococcus* species can get into the tonsils and cause sore throats or even enter the lungs or the brain and cause more serious effects.

Rod-shaped bacterium

Each one of your teeth can be covered by up to a billion individual bacteria.

MONSTROUS HABITAT

Microbes form a yellowish-white film called plaque that sticks to your teeth. Brushing gets rid of the plaque.

Round *Streptococcus* bacterium in the mouth

COMMON COLD

Ever heard of a rhinovirus? It's not something that affects big beasts of the African plains ... but it is the name for a group of microbes that can cause the common cold in humans. Achoo!

About 200 different viruses are responsible for colds and half of them are rhinoviruses. Rhino means "nose" and the nose certainly knows one of the first signs of getting a cold: more snot! Properly called **mucus**, this revolting substance does an important job. If a cold virus invades, the mucus carries defensive fighters called **antibodies** into battle.

Red blood cell

MONSTROUS DATA

Name	Common cold
Latin name	*Rhinovirus*
Adult length	30 nanometers
Habitat	Mouth, throat, lungs, nose
Lifespan	Its host's lifespan, or 15 minutes outside a host

A healthy person produces up to 1.5 liters of mucus a day.

In the US, around 22 million school days are missed each year because of colds.

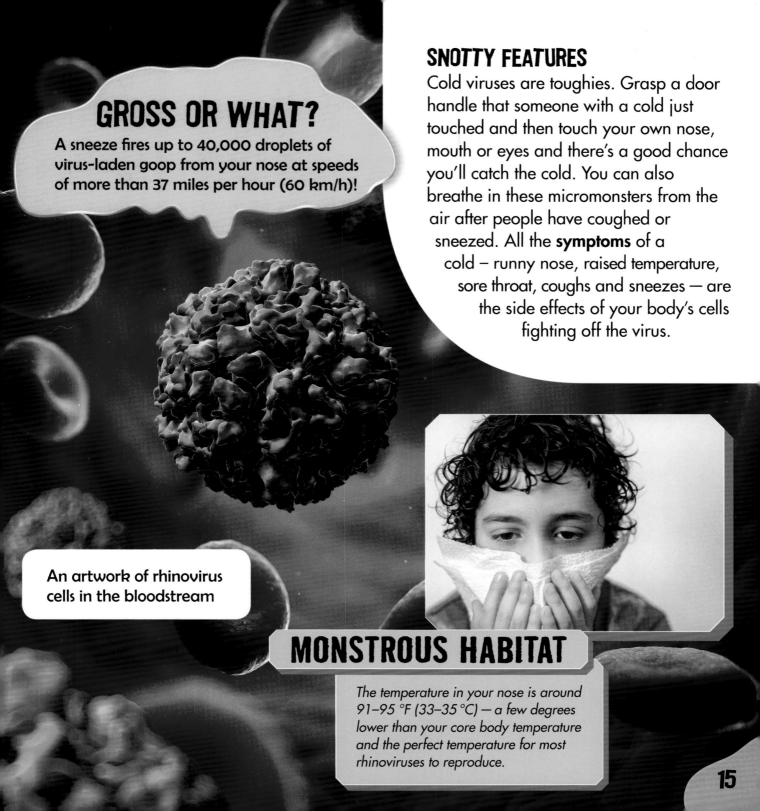

GROSS OR WHAT?

A sneeze fires up to 40,000 droplets of virus-laden goop from your nose at speeds of more than 37 miles per hour (60 km/h)!

SNOTTY FEATURES

Cold viruses are toughies. Grasp a door handle that someone with a cold just touched and then touch your own nose, mouth or eyes and there's a good chance you'll catch the cold. You can also breathe in these micromonsters from the air after people have coughed or sneezed. All the **symptoms** of a cold – runny nose, raised temperature, sore throat, coughs and sneezes — are the side effects of your body's cells fighting off the virus.

An artwork of rhinovirus cells in the bloodstream

MONSTROUS HABITAT

The temperature in your nose is around 91–95 °F (33–35 °C) — a few degrees lower than your core body temperature and the perfect temperature for most rhinoviruses to reproduce.

SKIN CRAWLERS

The human itch mite, also known as the scabies mite, is a micromonster that can live on your skin. If you're unlucky enough to catch scabies, you won't just play host to one bug, but to ten or more!

Scabies mites burrow into the skin to lay their eggs. They especially like warm crevices, such as those between your fingers, toes or buttocks! After a few days, the eggs hatch into six-legged larvae, which head straight into new, smaller burrows. Here, after a few more days, they molt and change into eight-legged nymphs. After two more molts, they reach their adult life stage. A female mite mates only once, but after that she can lay two or three eggs EVERY day for the rest of her life (about another six weeks). That's up to 126 eggs!

MONSTROUS DATA

Name	Scabies mite
Latin name	*Sarcoptes scabiei*
Adult length	0.4 mm (females); 0.2 mm (males)
Habitat	Human skin
Lifespan	6–8 weeks

MONSTROUS HABITAT

Mites usually move to a new host through skin-to-skin contact.

MITE-Y IRRITATING

The body usually reacts to the mites' burrowing, biting and poop with a fever and rash — and definitely some extreme itchiness. Symptoms don't usually appear for about a month. Special cream from the doctor will kill the scabies. To get rid of any lurkers, you have to wash all your pajamas, bedding and towels, and vacuum your carpets and furniture.

GROSS OR WHAT?

As well as ordinary scabies, there is crusted scabies. Infected people develop thick crusts of skin that contain THOUSANDS of mites and eggs.

Scabies mites are ancient — the ancient Egyptians had them at least 2,500 years ago, and they're mentioned in the Bible, too.

A scabies mite

THE ANTIMONSTER BRIGADE

Your body is home to an army of fighters—soldier cells ready to attack diseases or invading micromonsters. And the amazing thing about these soldier cells is that your body can make loads more of them whenever it needs to!

The proper name for these fighters is leukocytes or white blood cells. They travel from the bloodstream to wherever they're needed to destroy **pathogens** (disease-causing enemy cells). Some specialize in taking on fungi, bacteria or parasites. Others, called lymphocytes, battle viruses and **tumors**.

MONSTROUS HABITAT

Like all your blood cells, leukocytes are made right in the middle of your bones, in the soft, squishy marrow.

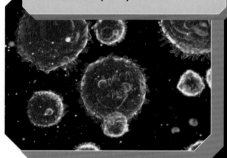

GROSS OR WHAT?

In 1796, Dr. Edward Jenner injected a boy with pus from cowpox sores. This sounds horrifying, but it was the first **vaccine**—fighting the pathogens protected the boy from a related but deadly disease, smallpox!

MONSTROUS DATA

Name	Leukocyte
Types	Neotrophil, eosiniophil, basophil, monocyte, lymphocyte
Adult length	10–15 micrometers
Habitat	Blood
Lifespan	Hours to years, depending on the type

A white blood cell (purple) engulfing superbug bacteria (yellow)

SUPER CELLS

White blood cells have two ways to destroy pathogens: "swallowing" them whole or making antibodies. If chicken pox pathogens invade your body, for example, your white blood cells produce antibodies to lock on to them and destroy them. If that pathogen invades your body again, you should be immune (safe from the disease) — most people don't catch chicken pox twice, for example! Vaccination is a clever way to make your body produce antibodies without you having to suffer a disease. The doctor gives you a very weak version of the dangerous pathogen.

The disease leukemia, which can be fatal, is caused when the body produces too many leukocytes.

White blood cells make up less than one percent of your blood.

Most people catch chicken pox as children — and then are immune from catching it ever again.

19

GOOD GUT FLORA

Your intestines are home to about 100 trillion microbes from up to 1,000 different species. Most are bacteria, but there are also other single-celled organisms and some fungi. Don't worry, though — these gut flora are goodies!

The micromonsters in your intestines have a safe place to live and plenty of food. In return, they help you to stay healthy. Some produce vital vitamins, such as vitamin B, which breaks down the **nutrients** in food, and vitamin K, which helps blood **clot**. Others produce **hormones** that tell your body how to store energy as fat. Many gut monsters also fight off harmful bacteria. Two "friendly" types of bacteria, also known as probiotics, are *Lactobacillus* and *Bifidus*.

MONSTROUS DATA

Name	Lactic acid bacteria
Latin name	*Lactobacillus*
Adult length	About 1 micrometer
Habitat	Mammals' intestines and some foods
Lifespan	Constantly dividing and multiplying

MONSTROUS HABITAT

*Probiotics are found in **fermented** foods, such as yogurt, sauerkraut (pickled cabbage) and pickles.*

20

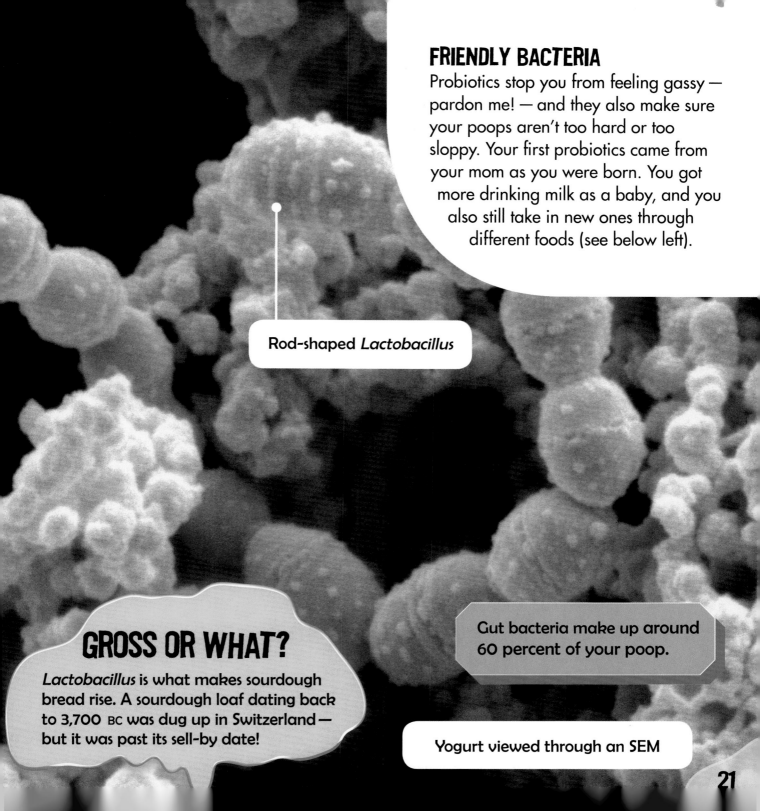

FRIENDLY BACTERIA

Probiotics stop you from feeling gassy — pardon me! — and they also make sure your poops aren't too hard or too sloppy. Your first probiotics came from your mom as you were born. You got more drinking milk as a baby, and you also still take in new ones through different foods (see below left).

Rod-shaped *Lactobacillus*

GROSS OR WHAT?

Lactobacillus is what makes sourdough bread rise. A sourdough loaf dating back to 3,700 BC was dug up in Switzerland — but it was past its sell-by date!

Gut bacteria make up around 60 percent of your poop.

Yogurt viewed through an SEM

TUMMY BUGS

Sometimes, nasty microbes get into your intestines. Viruses and parasites cause tummy bugs, but the worst culprits are bad bacteria that sneak into your body through food. They may be tiny, but these micromonsters can make for massive misery.

The main food poisoning baddies are *Campylobacter*, Salmonella, Listeria and *E. coli* (only six types of *E. coli* — most species are harmless). Once they reach your stomach, all these bacteria pass through its lining and start to destroy cells in the surrounding tissue. Salmonella has a sneaky trick. It uses a special **protein** as an "invisibility cloak." The protein stops any damage that would alert the body's white blood cells. This gives the Salmonella time to multiply into a mega-invasion force before it bursts through the stomach walls.

MONSTROUS HABITAT

*Raw or undercooked meat can contain harmful bacteria. So can eggs, **unpasteurized** cheese and even fruit and vegetables.*

The 2011 outbreak of *E. coli* in Europe, traced back to alfalfa from an organic farm, killed more than fifty people and made thousands more very ill.

Around 48 million people get food poisoning in the US each year—that's one in 6.

GROSS OR WHAT?

To find out what microbe is causing food poisoning, a doctor has to take a sample of your blood—and a sample of your poop, too!

Salmonella bacteria (red) invading human cells

MONSTROUS DATA

Name	Salmonella
Latin name	*Salmonella bongori* or *Salmonella enterica*
Adult length	2–5 micrometers
Habitat	Animals and the environment
Lifespan	Constantly dividing and multiplying

SICK SYMPTOMS

Food poisoning can last up to two weeks. While your soldier cells (see pages 18–19) fight off the invaders, you suffer from nausea, vomiting, stomach cramps and disgusting diarrhea. You lose water in all those runny poops, so you may also have fever, headaches and dizziness (all signs of dehydration, or not taking in enough water).

TINY WORMS

Imagine looking into the toilet and seeing wriggling white worms in your poop. It sounds like the stuff of nightmares! In the US, around 11 percent of children have pinworms by the age of ten!

Pinworms are also called threadworms because they look like little strands of white thread. If you get them, they will lay teeny-tiny eggs inside your bottom, adding a coating of mucus to make you feel especially itchy. Don't scratch! You'll pick up some of the tiny eggs under your fingernails and pass them on to other people — or back into your own body.

Pinworms lay about 11,000 eggs around their host's bottom.

MONSTROUS HABITAT

Pinworms live in human digestive systems — but their eggs are often found under fingernails. Sucking your fingers allows any eggs to enter your body. Shudder!

You can catch pinworms by breathing in their eggs.

GROSS OR WHAT?

You can get rid of worms by taking a special medicine that **paralyzes** them so they can't lay eggs. The bad news is, it turns your poop orange or red!

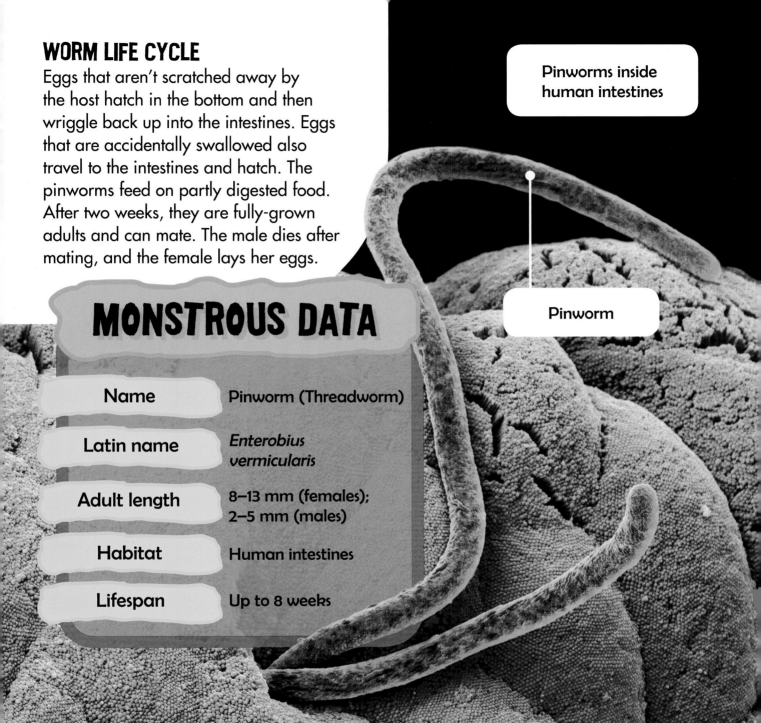

WORM LIFE CYCLE

Eggs that aren't scratched away by the host hatch in the bottom and then wriggle back up into the intestines. Eggs that are accidentally swallowed also travel to the intestines and hatch. The pinworms feed on partly digested food. After two weeks, they are fully-grown adults and can mate. The male dies after mating, and the female lays her eggs.

Pinworms inside human intestines

Pinworm

MONSTROUS DATA

Name	Pinworm (Threadworm)
Latin name	*Enterobius vermicularis*
Adult length	8–13 mm (females); 2–5 mm (males)
Habitat	Human intestines
Lifespan	Up to 8 weeks

FOOT FUNGUS

Don't expect to see mushrooms sprouting between your toes if you catch athlete's foot. It *is* caused by tiny fungi spreading over your skin — but it just looks like a scaly rash.

Several different kinds of fungus cause athlete's foot, all known as dermatophytes. Despite their name (*dermatos* means "skin" and *phyte* means "plant"), these micromonsters are fungi, not plants. They like to live in warm, moist places, such as between your toes or inside stinky, old sneakers. They spread over the top layer of the skin, feeding on dead cells. They also push their rootlike **hyphae** into any cuts or cracks in the skin and this can lead to painful infections.

MONSTROUS HABITAT

*Fungi **spores** can lie dormant in sneakers or on changing room floors for years.*

MONSTROUS DATA

Name	Athlete's foot
Latin name	*Trichophyton*
Hyphae length	2–10 micrometers
Habitat	Skin
Lifespan	Forever without antifungal treatment

GROSS OR WHAT?

Young men are worst affected by athlete's foot, especially if they sweat a lot and never change their socks!

The fungi that cause athlete's foot are also responsible for another nasty and very itchy skin problem — ringworm.

Pets can get dermatophytes —
so if you're treating yourself,
remember to treat Fido, too!

Trichophyton, one of the fungi
that can cause athlete's foot,
seen through an SEM. The
orange blobs are its spores.

Feet infected by
athlete's foot

HIGH JUMPERS

Despite its name, the human flea isn't too fussy about what it lives on — it's just as happy on birds and other mammals as people. Its only requirement is that its host is warm-blooded, because this vampire of the insect world feeds on blood.

Fleas have four stages in their life: egg, larva, **pupa** and adult. Like all insects, they start out as an egg. After three or four days, this hatches into a wriggling larva. The larva's preferred food is even more disgusting than its parents' — it eats poop from adult fleas!

GROSS OR WHAT?

Human fleas famously carried the bacteria responsible for a terrible disease called the plague, or Black Death, that wiped out more than half the people in Europe during the 1300s.

A female flea lays more than 5,000 eggs during her lifetime.

MONSTROUS DATA

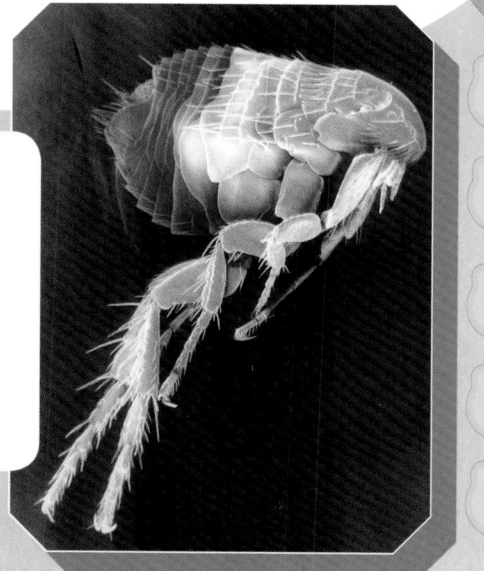

Relative to their size, fleas are one of the animal world's highest jumpers, able to leap as high as 7 inches (18 cm).

Name	Human flea
Latin name	*Pulex irritans*
Adult length	1.5–4 mm
Habitat	Skin
Lifespan	2–3 months as an adult

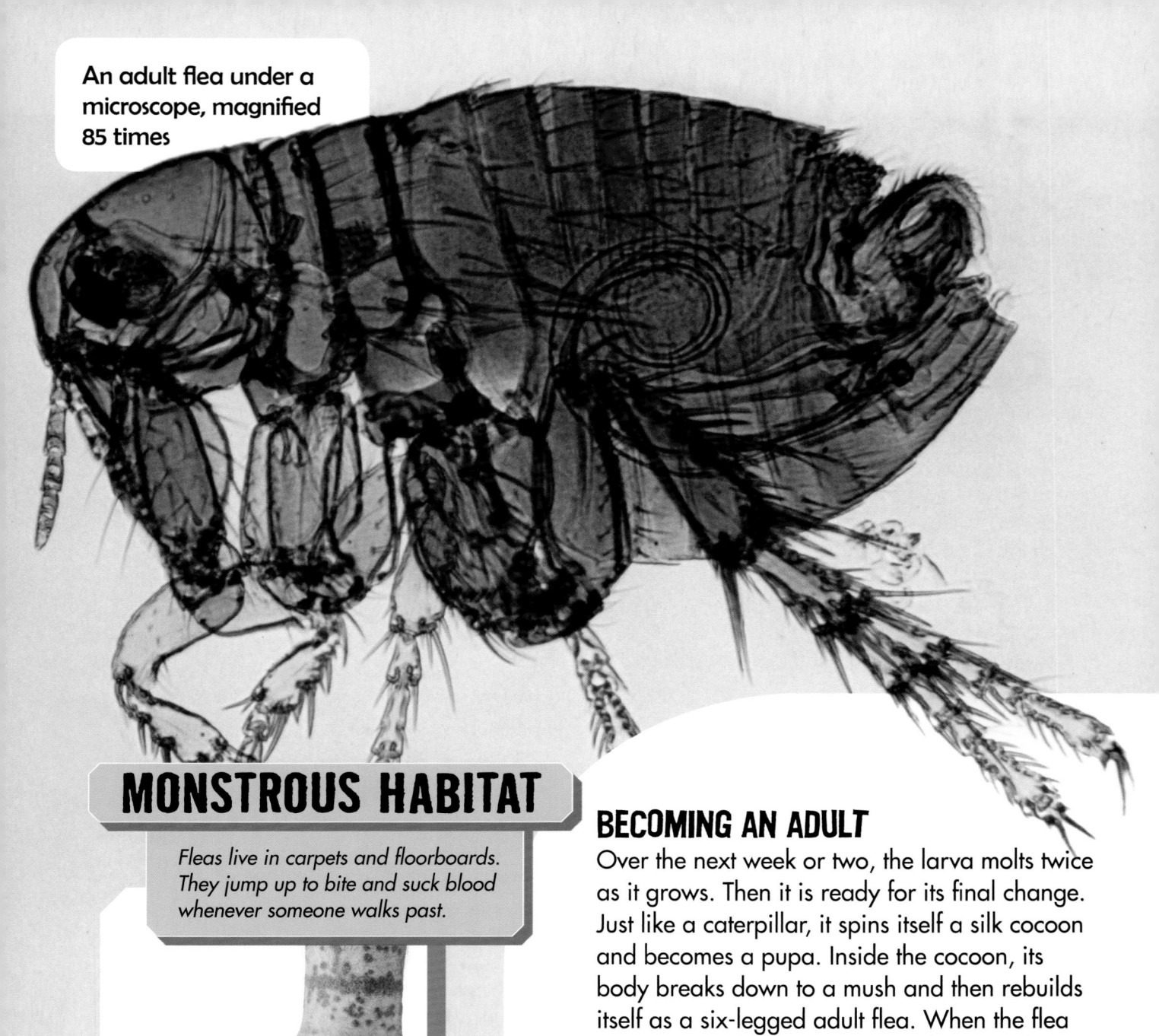

An adult flea under a microscope, magnified 85 times

MONSTROUS HABITAT

Fleas live in carpets and floorboards. They jump up to bite and suck blood whenever someone walks past.

BECOMING AN ADULT

Over the next week or two, the larva molts twice as it grows. Then it is ready for its final change. Just like a caterpillar, it spins itself a silk cocoon and becomes a pupa. Inside the cocoon, its body breaks down to a mush and then rebuilds itself as a six-legged adult flea. When the flea senses a suitable host nearby, it leaps and lands — and uses its piercing mouthparts to suck up its first sip of blood. If it doesn't find a blood meal within a week, it dies.

GLOSSARY

antibody any protein made by an animal to defend against invading microbes

bacterium (pl: bacteria) a one-celled organism that is the most numerous living thing in the world. An example is the food-poisoning bug Salmonella.

cell the tiny unit that living things are made of

clot to form a solid mass. Clotting stops blood loss after an injury.

fermented made to bubble and change chemically because of the actions of yeast

fungus (pl: fungi) an organism that lives on and feeds off live or dead organic matter and reproduces with spores. Mushrooms and mildew are both fungi.

gland a part of the body that releases chemical substances

habitat the place or type of place where an organism usually lives

hormone a substance released by a gland that sends instructions to particular cells or tissues

host an organism that is home to a parasite or a cell that is home to a virus

hypha (pl: hyphae) one of the threads that some fungi use to grow and spread on their host

infestation an invasion of lots of parasites

intestines also called the bowels, the part of the digestive system between the stomach and the anus

larva (pl: larvae) the immature, wingless and wormlike form of an insect that hatches from an egg and later completely changes inside a pupa

mate to come together to breed (produce offspring)

microbe any microscopic living thing that is not an animal

micrometer the measurement of length that is one-thousandth of a millimeter and sometimes called a micron

microorganism a living thing too small to see without a microscope

mucus moist, slippery spit or snot

nanometer the measurement of length that is one-millionth of a millimeter

nutrient a substance in food that provides organisms with what they need to survive and grow

nymph the immature, wingless form of an insect that hatches from an egg and later partly changes by developing wings inside a pupa

paralyze to make a living thing unable to move

parasite a living thing that lives on or in another living thing and uses its host as food

pathogen a microorganism, such as a bacterium, that causes disease

protein one of a group of chemicals that help build body tissue

pupa (pl: pupae) the hard cover that surrounds a larva or nymph while it changes into its adult form

reproduce produce offspring

species a group of similar organisms that can mate and produce offspring

spore a plant or fungus cell that develops into a new plant or fungus

symptom a sign of a disease or condition

tumor an abnormal lump of cells growing on or in the body

unpasteurized describes milk or cheese that has not been pasteurized. Pasteurization is heating and cooling milk in order to kill any microbes in it.

vaccine a weakened form of a pathogen introduced into the body to boost its defenses

virus a microbe that multiplies by infecting the cells of organisms

FURTHER INFORMATION

Books

Complete Book of the Microscope
by Kirsteen Rogers (Usborne, 2012)

Disgusting and Dreadful Science:
Smelly Farts and Other Body Horrors
by Anna Claybourne (Franklin Watts, 2014)

Horrible Science: Microscopic Monsters
by Nick Arnold (Scholastic, 2014)

Your Growling Guts and Dynamic Digestive System
by Paul Mason (Franklin Watts, 2015)

Websites

PowerKids Press has developed an online list of websites related to the subject of this book. This site is updated regularly. Please use this link to access the list:
www.powerkidslinks.com/mm/body

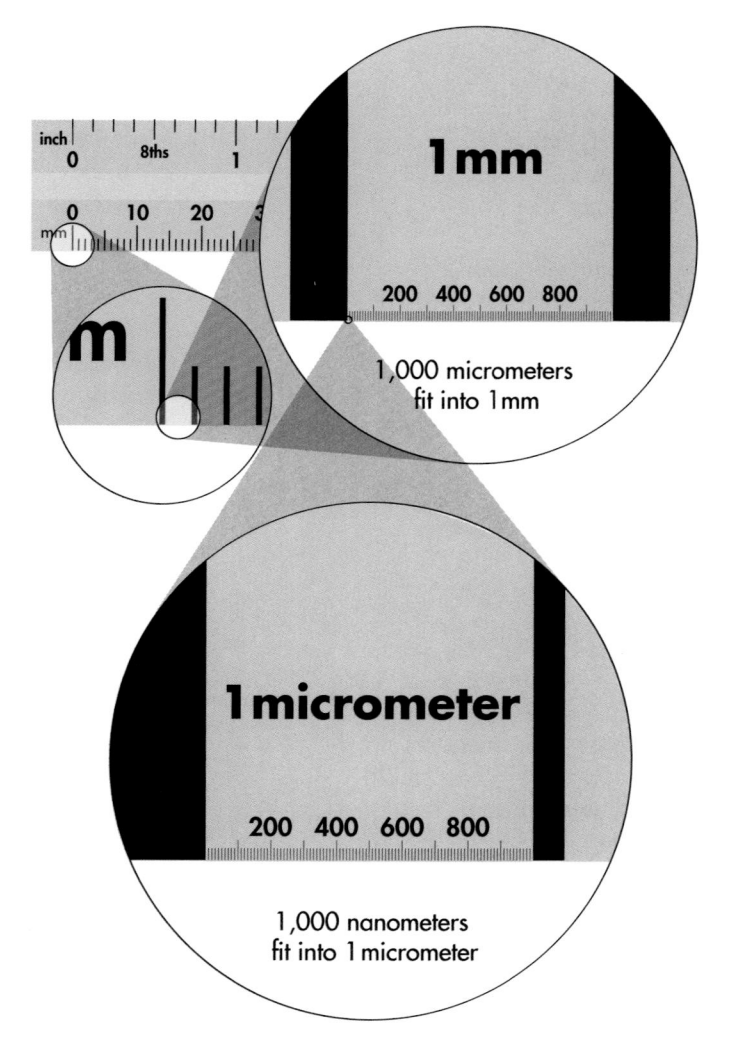

1,000 micrometers
fit into 1mm

1,000 nanometers
fit into 1 micrometer

Measuring the microscopic world

It's hard to imagine how small micrometers and nanometers really are. This picture helps you to see how they compare to a millimeter. Millimeters are pretty tiny themselves, but they are GIANT compared to nanometers. In every millimeter, there are one million nanometers!

INDEX